POEMS ON LOVE, LIFE, AND RELATIONSHIPS

Free to Be Me

CHERRIE AMOUR

Free to be Me: Poems on Love, Life, and Relationships.
© 2013 by C.A. Woods. All rights reserved. Printed in the United States of America. No part of this book may be reproduced in any form or by any electronic or mechanical means, including information storage and retrieval systems, without permission in writing from the author, except by a reviewer who may quote brief passages in a review.

Cover Design: Noumenon Designs

Contact Cherrie Amour at
cherrieamourpoet@gmail.com

WWW.CHERRIEAMOUR.COM

ISBN 978-0-615-87817-1

This book is dedicated to Newton Howe (my uncle) who passed away in June 2012; my sister Wendy; and my family of friends who helped me on my journey to loving me: Admiral, Aunty Cynthia, Corn, Denny, Pat, Ruben and Sonya. I love you all.

CONTENTS

FOREWORD 3
For Uncle Newton 5

LIVIN'
Livin' 8
Why I Write 9
A Conversation with Grandma 10
Old Soul 11
1971 - The Lady from England 12
A New Beginning 13
Hermoso Negro 14
Love Lessons 16
Freedom 18
My Journey 19
Spoken Words 21
Losing Louella (My Sister) 23
Ode to My Mother 24
Sad 26
Emptiness 27
The Secret 28
The Best Gift 29
Sitting Still 30

LOVIN'

Lovin'	32
I Don'T	33
What I Want	35
What Love Ain't	36
Fyah	38
Six Figures	39
Near Miss	41
Ouch!	43
Hopeful Romantic	44
"In" Love	45
Men and Love	46
What Love Is	47
My Love	48
RFP	49
This Morning	50

ACKNOWLEDGEMENTS 53

Foreword

Having known Cherrie for more than a decade, reading this intimate collection of poetry is akin to seeing a director's cut of film vignettes in which I played a recurring cameo role. Learning more about her childhood and primordial losses puts so much into context. In the late 1990s, her Toronto and my Tokyo circles linked and, a few years later, when we both landed as strangers in the strange land of my hometown of Detroit, we fell into an easy kinship as expat and repatriated citizens of the global village, patrons of the arts and love-longing single thirtysomethings. Open. Wistful. Vulnerable. Hopeful.

Until reading this book, I presumed her poetic persona's name was her own invention and a clever turn on the Stevie Wonder song. In discovering that the Cherrie Amour moniker was one first given her by "The Lady from England," whom she first met as an 8-year-old in 1971, (soon after the song's 1969 release), the lyrics take on a sadly ironic resonance.

My Cherie Amour, lovely as a summer's day
My Cherie Amour, distant as the Milky Way
My Cherie Amour, pretty little one that I adore
You're the only girl my heart beats for
How I wish that you were mine

The young mother who entrusted Cherrie and her siblings to her mother-in-law while she migrated to England to better herself and the family's lot surely longed for her "pretty little one" certainly as much as the child ached for her. But in making this practical calculation, she probably never imagined the sacrifice it really entailed. Broken bonds that left an indelible mark. A chasm of years never to be spanned.

You're the only girl my heart beats for
How I wish that you were mine

After spending years in the gallery crowds or as a face in the audience at the poetry slams and music venues of the underground Detroit arts scene of the 2000s, I was surprised and impressed to witness the emergence of Cherrie Amour, the performance artist.

Ongoing from stage to page, Cherrie said: "It's different putting things in writing. When you perform, people might remember a verse or two, but when you write it in a book, it's more permanent."

This Caribbean flower has blossomed in the cold, sometimes unyielding soil of her adopted U.S. homeland. She is brave, bold and generous in letting us in on this journey to self, to family, to love and back home.

-Sonya Vann, Editor

For Uncle Newton

(Who died on June 12, 2012)

Well read, six feet tall, and strong-minded
I remember our long phone conversations
On many topics.

World politics, the state of museums and international trade
I often wondered when and where a man who spent his life in Trinidad
Developed the interests you had?

When I asked you about almost anything
When my world became vague and unsure
You always had an answer or a position.

Our long talks on my international phone line
Taught me many things about human nature
And that I needed to focus on what I wanted.

And that spending too much time
Trying to understand a situation or a person
Was time I could spend doing something more productive.

I liked your clear definitions
And your life's map
You had very little room for vagueness and pauses.

Your life was tight but not closed
Rigid and yet permeable
You mixed contradictions in a way that worked.

I admired your convictions
Even when I didn't agree

And the time you gave me to share my thoughts.

And though your physical self is no more
Your presence and spirit live on...
In my heart.

Livin'

LIVIN'

Some days....
I walk heavy with pain
My head in a storm
Weighed down by rain.

Where are the days of my joy?
Where are my moments of laughter?
Where are my missing friends?
Where is the love I am after?

But then rain subsides
The sun breaks through
And like from night to day
My dark thoughts go away.

My sadness becomes joy
Heaviness seems lighter
The sun comes out
Making my day brighter.

WHY I WRITE

I pull the stories out of my head
And put them on paper
So I can really see them and

Determine what in my life
is real or fiction.
What characters are living in my head?
Which ones dominate without a right?
Which ones cower in the corner in fear?

What is murky?
What is clear?
What is shallow?
What looms profound?

And by inscribing them onto a page
I give myself permission to live.

A Conversation with Grandma

Today I asked my grandmother
"Do I have a mother and father?

She looked me in the eye and said,
"Look at that picture on the wall."

I looked at the picture of a handsome light-skinned man in a white shirt
He is tall and handsome with a stern look.

She said, "That is your father, he is at school in England."

"But what about my mother" I asked?

She paused, looked up at the ceiling, and muttered under her breath
"She is in England too, but she should be here."

Then she looked me dead in the eye and said, "I am your mother."

OLD SOUL

I was raised by my grandparents
"I'm an old soul," some would say
They taught me to live
The old "*fashion*" way.

They spoke to me about the "gift" of patience
And to carry myself with pride
And when life presents challenges
Look to God as my guide.

They taught me to be disciplined
To first listen ... in order to hear
And that through the stresses of life
I must forge on, through my fears.

They taught me the power of words
And to stand firm for what I believe
And that life's experiences if handled well
Will give me positive stories to tell.

So yes I'm an old soul
I know my grandparents would be proud
Their teachings are my life's compass
And help me stand out from the crowd.

1971 - THE LADY FROM ENGLAND

The Lady from England
Holds my face between her hands
"My sweet little girl," she says
As she hugs me with her chubby arms

She steps back a few steps
Examines me from head to toe
"I can't believe how you've grown in six years," she says.
I look at her wanting her to go.

Back to where she came from
Just leave me alone
I feel confused
And I want her gone.

"Don't you remember me, Cherrie Amour?" She says
I back away and shake my head no
She reaches her hand out to me
I close my eyes wishing she would go.

She takes small steps towards me
And pulls my head to her chest
I feel her body shaking and moisture in my hair
I give in and let my body rest.

I'm not sure what to do
I feel suffocated and smothered
I do not like her
This lady from England, my mother.

A New Beginning

We arrived in Canada
Five children and one mother
In 1972.

HERMOSO NEGRO

(Honorable Mention Winner of the 2013 Allan Ginsberg Poetry Awards)

"Hermoso Negro," my Dad would say
As he pulled the hairs from his chin with a tweezer
I would watch him move his face closer to the mirror in the bathroom
"Hermoso Negro," he would say again.

Handsome black man, I guess that's how my Dad saw himself
Or that's what he said
And when he visited my school on parents/teachers night
My female teachers acted like he was handsome.

6' 2", not so dark-skinned with a strong Caribbean accent
A professional man
My Dad was a novelty at my school in Dartmouth, Nova Scotia.

"Mr. Woods, you look like Harry Belafonte," my home room teacher said
My dad would respond with a toothy grin.

He would set up conferences with my teachers
To ask if I should watch soap operas
The merits of reading fiction books
What my appropriate bedtime should be.

I often wondered if my teachers understood most of what he was saying
Because at no time did he ever try to conceal his Caribbean accent.

I remember being embarrassed in front of my friends
When he would say "tree" for three, "glass" for window
"How ya going?" instead of How are you?
But he always spoke unapologetically.

That part I liked.

LOVE LESSONS

My Dad worked the afternoon shift
So he was mostly gone after school
And mostly asleep, when we got ready for school.

My mother was a nurse
And from what I heard
An exceptional and bright one.

On the days, my father woke early
My mother served him breakfast on a tray
As he sat watching TV with his feet up on the coffee table.

"Is the food okay," my mother would ask?
"Do you need anything else?"
Most times he would quickly glance at her and then turn back to the TV
"It's okay," he would say in a matter-of-fact voice.

The sad expression on my mother's face
Seemed to say, be kind to me
But I don't know if she ever asked him to.

When my Dad was at work
My mom was confident and bossy.

"Wait till your Dad gets home!"
She would shout
When we didn't do what she wanted.

Then when Dad got home
She would wake the guilty child
And report their latest transgression

And my father would punish them

And my mom would smile
At whichever one of us cried.

So I learned from my mother
That women should cater to men
And men do not always thank them.

I learned that a love relationship
Meant I could be strong in my job
But not at home.

I'm beginning to realize though
That I am not my mother
And love can be good.

FREEDOM

Left home at eighteen
On my own and afraid
But needing to breathe.

My Journey

I'm on a journey
To help me love myself
And I want some company for this trip.

Cause I have a lot of baggage
That I want to let go
But I've had it for so long
A lot of it I know.

To give up my life pattern and begin to make a change
Is not something that is easy
In fact it all feels strange.

I feel lost and all alone
And I want to feel renewed
And begin to walk a new path
And find the self-love that I am due.

But how do I create
A new road map for my life?
How do I mentally let go
Of all my stress and strife?

I have done the self-reflection work
That has helped me to see
That some of my beliefs
Are not as true as I thought them to be

And even though I want to be in a better emotional place
I will have to do a lot of changing
To get to a better mental space.

I look to friends for support
I want someone to guide me

But how can they give me advice
When I hide the real me.

To really share who I am
Comes with a lot of fear
How do I get past my pretense?
How do I make the world hear?

My journey to inner peace
On this often lonely road
Will lead me to a better place
And help me reduce my load.

I'm committed to easing my pain
And though it's not any fun
I have to stop grasping
And holding on to anyone.

As time passes I stop grasping
I let myself feel fear
When I feel overwhelmed
I fall to my knees in prayer.

Now my fear is lessening
And I'm on more solid ground
I will keep moving forward
On my journey to the unbound.

SPOKEN WORDS

I read a poem about my mother today
In front of a group of twenty other writers
Novelists, mystery writers, non-fiction writers,
religious writers and poets.

My palms were sweaty
My heart beat fast
And my stomach churned round and round.

I kept my eyes lowered
And focused on reading the poem
I tried to keep my voice even though my knees were shaking.

I shared the story of my childhood
Of my mother leaving myself and my siblings,
For six years to study in England with my father.

About her not being able to love me as I needed when she returned
Her infrequent hugs and kisses
Her many punishments and rules.

I read about my pain and emotional neglect
And as I read, my voice got stronger, and bigger
Because everything I read was the truth.

I read it and felt it – the disappointment and the loss
The neediness that I still feel as an adult
Then I stopped and looked up and out at the audience.

Afraid to walk back to my chair
Because my legs felt rubbery and unsteady
I stayed at the podium for another two minutes.

As I stood at the podium frozen in that spot
I looked up slowly and tentatively
At the silent audience.

I saw tears on some faces
Others had a somber look
Some heads shook from left to right.

Were those tears for the many broken daughters?

LOSING LOUELLA (MY SISTER)

When Louella died
Life stopped making sense.
And I began to question everything
And the world didn't feel safe anymore.

Getting out of bed in the morning felt pointless
Getting dressed to go to work took a long time
And every time I stepped outside my door
I felt like I would die too.

That some drunk driver would hit me
Or I would have a heart attack while sleeping
Or while at my bank withdrawing cash from my account
A bank robber would kill everyone in the building.

My sister Louella
The vibrant, dynamic one who lived a full life
Traveled at the drop of a hat
And had closets full of clothes for future pregnancies.

My sister Louella
Who did what she wanted
And upon graduating from university at 19
Returned to her *true* home--Trinidad.

I remember getting her last email
About her plans to travel
Her plans to do dialysis from home
Her plans to not let lupus win.

But lupus got greedy again
And took her heart, after taking her lungs and kidneys
And eight years later
Life still doesn't make sense.

ODE TO MY MOTHER

"Swing low, sweet chariot
Coming for to carry her home."*

My mother is no longer with us
She is now laid to rest
My siblings and I
We did our best
To bring respect and honor to her passing.

And then I went home
And I slept.

Slept away the disappointment of knowing she never
loved me as I needed
Slept away the intimacy that I still seek with myself
Slept away the pain
Slept away the fear
Slept away the disappointment
Of knowing she can no longer hear
The nights I cried and needed her to see
That I am me.

I wish I could feel anger
But all I feel is sadness
I wish I could feel something good
But I must first sort through the madness
Of the life I now must lead
Truly strong and very real
I can no longer live in a fantasy
That one day my family will be
Together, laughing, loving and free.

I slept away the baggage
Placed on me and my siblings from birth
And the spirits that were broken

By words degrading our worth.

And now I know
The truth will set you free
But free to be whom?
Free to be me.

(* excerpt from hymn, Swing Low Sweet Chariot)

SAD

I don't want to be sad
I don't want to live in a place
Where darkness surrounds me
And everything seems far away.

I don't want to be sad
I don't want to be buried in my thoughts
To have conversations with myself, and within myself.

I don't want to be sad
I don't want to be self-consumed
Thinking, planning and analyzing.

I don't want to be sad
I want to walk in the sunlight
Accept life for what it is
And when someone criticizes me (for being me)
I want to shout, I DON'T CARE!

I don't want to be sad
I just want to appreciate
Art, reading, writing, music and laughter
And feel that I am alright with me.

EMPTINESS

There is emptiness in my soul
That keeps me from true contentment
It keeps me wanting even when I have it all
It keeps me seeking even though I've found my worth.

It comes from missed love from my childhood
And though I've had lots of love since
It seems like the emptiness is like a bottomless well
The more I get the more I want.

I've learned that love
Is like the seasons
It has its cycles and changes
Sometimes hot, sometimes cold.

Spring comes and the grass begins to slowly grow
Summer, the grass becomes lush and plentiful
In fall it begins to wither
Then in winter the grass becomes dormant.

I hope one day, my soul no longer feels empty
But more like that grassy field that changes with the seasons
And I will know that regardless of love's highs and lows
It will always return to spring.

THE SECRET

Wish someone had told me that one little secret
That it seems everyone knows but me

That one secret
Could have kept me from years of distress and dissatisfaction

Someone finally told me
That one little secret.

I control my own happiness.

THE BEST GIFT

I traveled five hours on an international flight
To get the best gift I'll ever receive
It took 48 years to get this gift.

I've prayed for it, asked for it, been a good person for it
Endured rejection, depression
Tried to get it from random souls!

I had to travel over 2,000 miles for it...

My father apologized for not acknowledging my worth
Face to face!
And he listened to what I had to say...really listened.

SITTING STILL

I need to sit still
I need to sit still
I need to sit still
I need to sit still.

My friends say at this point
In my life
That it's time to sit still.

I say, "How do I slow down?"
My mind is wired to go round and round
Can I stop by sheer force of will?

I practice daily
To live life day to day
Trying not to control
By the things I say.

"Let life take its course"
My wise friends often tell
Me to chill, sit back and allow
Life to gel.

I am sitting still
I am sitting still
I am sitting still
I am sitting still.

Lovin'

Lovin'

For a long time
 I didn't understand romantic love.

I spent a lot of time
Chasing it
Crying over it
Thinking I would die for it.

Losing sleep
Counting sheep
Running from it
Wanting it.

Then when I did get it
I spent a lot of time trying to own it
Control it
Analyze it
And sanitize it.

And now, I know to let it grow
Set it free
And just learn to love me.

I Don't

On our wedding day
As we stood at the altar
I looked into your eyes and said, "I do."
Though I wasn't sure I did.

But there I stood in my white wedding dress
Willing myself to be happy.
And as friends and family hugged us in the receiving line
I knew that we would part before death.

Because at that moment
I knew my fear and emotional pain
Could not, would not, withstand the demands and requirements
Of your love.

And I realized that you being happy and light-hearted
Could not, would not mend my unhealed and unresolved childhood pain
And that no white picket fence life
Could heal my emotional wounds.

When you hugged and kissed me
I tried hard to reciprocate.
But your kisses made me feel suffocated
And your hugs felt like chains wrapped around my body.

And all I could think was, "How can I make this stop?"
"How can I make you go away?"
Before you realize that
I could not, would not be able to love you back.

And so I argued and threw things

I yelled and screamed and tailored my words as
weapons against you.
I left you no choice but to ask me,
"Do you want me to leave?"

And I said, "I do."
And you did.

What I Want

What I want and what I fear
Are the same thing
To be loved.

What Love Ain't

For the first time in my life
After all the pain and strife
I finally get it!

"Get what," you ask?
Well ... I finally grasp what love ain't.

I've been in all kinds of love okay
"Really", you say?

Yes, I've been in:
Oooh he's so fine love
Wish he were mine love
Can't sleep love
Can't eat love
Can't breathe love
Can't think love
I need a drink love
It hurts all the time love
Why can't he be mine love?

He completes me love
He defeats me love
Superstar love
Can't be who you are love.

Love is not possession
Love is not pain
Love is not forced
Love is not for financial gain
Love is a part
Love is not all of your heart.
Love has its highs and lows
Love is not physical blows.

So what!!! You ask?
Well ... I finally grasp.

That love is not always about somebody else
Love really starts with self.

FYAH

Our love is like fyah
Our love is like fyah
Red, orange, yellow — bright
Scorching, intense, burning
Full of flame and fight.

Our love is like fyah
Our love is like fyah
Exciting, hot like a candle flame
Destroying, igniting, encasing
This is love by any other name.

Our love is like fyah
Our love is like fyah
It captivates me in every way
Encircling my soul
Confusing my whole
Being
Until it dies and leaves me cold.

SIX FIGURES

He ordered our dinner
Clearly he forgot to ask
If I might want to do it for myself
His arrogance was hard to grasp.

This was our first date
And he only spoke about himself
He never asked about me
Like an unread book on a shelf.

He said, "I make six figures."
"How nice!" I replied.
Smiling, I thought,
"That does not entice."

He added, "I have two degrees — an undergrad and a grad."
"How impressive!" I commented.
But I thought, "How sad."
His M.O. is based on acquiring dough.

"Six figures!" I thought
"Does he believe I can be bought?"
"He's a check that won't bounce!" my girlfriend announced.
"Think suburbs, think houses, and think sports cars."
"He may be able to buy you," I said.
"But character, honesty and respect are what I value."

So farewell, Six Figures
Please no hard feelings
There are others out there
Who will find you appealing.

I'll hold out for substance

And someone more deep
Money and education are great
But kindness, integrity and caring
Are things that will keep.

NEAR MISS

Near Miss
Even when we kiss
And my head spins and I see fireworks and stars
I am still Venus
And you are still Mars.

Near miss
And though it feels like we are pieces of the same puzzle
We still do not fit
And though like magnets we're drawn together
Still, I must admit
That we are not birds of a feather.

Near Miss
My passion, the things that I love
You know but don't share
Do you even care?
Outside your head?
Outside your bed?

Near miss
I love movies
We've shared that twice or maybe once
Still, you give your love by the ounce
Do I need to bounce?
Near miss
You live in a box
I like the freedom to grow
You like control
I let my seeds sow.

Near miss
Even though I care

Neither one of us is really there
Let's just call this what it is
A near miss.

Ouch!

When he walked into the poetry show
Thoughts started to flow ... into my mind.

Ooooooo Weeeeeeeee! He is a FINE tall glass of hot chocolate!

I wanted to drink from that glass right away
I couldn't and wouldn't wait for the break of day.

And so...I got burnt?

Ouch!

And all of that steam
Definitely fogged up my brain
And my fantasy dream
Blocked memories of past lessons of pain.

Cause, usually I appreciate, but still wait
And not leap before I look.
I judged the cover, not the book
And now I'm sad as rain

Cause...I got burnt...

Ouch!

But upon reflection
And some introspection
I realize if I was wise
I should've, could've waited...for him
That tall FINE glass of hot chocolate...
To cool down before I touched.

HOPEFUL ROMANTIC

I'm a hopeful romantic
I love walks in the moonlight
Love songs and candlelit dinners
Holding hands
Piggy back rides
And slow succulent kisses.

I'm a hopeful romantic
I have dreams of vacations on tropical islands
Sitting under palm trees
Slowly sipping piña coladas
Sucking on sun-ripened mangoes
And watching dancers gyrate under a limbo stick.

I'm a hopeful romantic ...
I have visions of you and me
Jumping the broom on the shores of Barbados
Of you lifting me effortlessly over the threshold
Then tossing me on a four-poster bed covered in mosquito netting
And loving me until 5 a.m. in the morning.

I'm a hopeful romantic
I hope that romance is not dead
That courting is not a lost art
That there is still some excitement in delayed gratification.

"IN" LOVE

I know how to start love
And how to end love
It's the middle I have the most problems with.

MEN AND LOVE

A 71-year old Santa Claus
Told me that when men love
They are like jello
And that the modern-day woman
Takes that jello
And washes it down the sink drain
Instead of savoring it
Enjoying its softness and bounce
And valuing its flavor.

What Love Is

I used to think that when love came
There would be fireworks, announcements, stars, excitement
And complete euphoria!
And things would go smoothly.

But then you came along
With your stuff, lots of stuff
Your commitments, history, unavailability, limitations
Your reluctance, rationalizations, and compartmentalization
But also with your joie de vivre, excitement, conversation, laughter
Playfulness, affection, hugs, kisses, strength and intelligence.

Now I know that love can come
With no warning, no announcement
Not simple, but complicated
Seeping into my skin
Satisfying my hunger
Not to be controlled, only accepted.

MY LOVE

My love has...
Boundaries
And conditions
Rules
Limits
And
Sections
Heart
Passion
Pain
Joy
Sorrow
Excitement
Sadness
Closeness
And Distance
Me
And you?

RFP

I want a love that has faith
A love based on spiritual strength
A love that has words that say what is meant
A love that doesn't hurry, a love that can wait.

I want a love that stays
Stays through the good and the bad
Through the happy and sad
Through the bright and dark days.

I want a love that will grow
Grow in its depth and understanding
A love that is strong but not demanding
A love that I can know.

I want a love that is real
No façades, no pretense
An authentic love that makes good sense
A love that I can feel.

I want a love that is strong
That can stand the test of time
A love that has rhythm and rhyme
A love where I feel I belong.

This Morning

I saw you this morning when we woke up
Without my rose-colored glasses

I saw a man ---flesh and blood
With faults and mistakes and uncertainties
Trying to do the best he can...
And not always getting it right.

Doing his best to keep me happy
And quiet.
To not over promise and under deliver
Trying to keep things real and honest.

And I see me, wanting you to move faster
Get things done faster
Love me faster, figure things out faster
And to save me, nurture me and take care of me.

As if I couldn't
As if I haven't done good
By myself, and for myself.

But now I see you
With my almost 20/20 vision
Just flesh and blood
Not a knight in shining armor
Doing the best you can
Trying to be the best man
You can be.

So now, I've stored my rose-colored glasses
In the back of my desk drawer.

ACKNOWLEDGEMENTS

I thank God for helping me in this continuous and challenging journey called life, and for helping me find enjoyment despite the challenges.

I thank the City of Detroit for revealing the artist in me and for its strong, supportive artists' community.

I thank my parents Reginald Woods and Rachel Woods (nee Howe – who passed away in 2008); for giving me the best that they could.

I thank Geno, my artistic brother who helps me understand how demanding and yet fulfilling being an artist can be.

I thank Denny Hunte for reviewing my work and for being a friend for 25 years (with some breaks) and for understanding and clarifying life, when I can't.

I thank my brother David Woods for taking the time to review my work and for being an amazing artistic role model. Your success as a poet, visual artist and curator is inspiring.

I thank Sonya Vann, who wrote my foreword, for being consistent, calm, kind and observant when I was floundering, emotional, and unclear.

I thank Black Writers Guild of Maryland members for providing me with the knowledge and confidence to take this book from an idea to a reality.

I thank all readers for supporting this book.

ABOUT THE AUTHOR

Poet, Cherrie Amour was born in Trinidad, W.I. and immigrated to Canada at the age of eight with her siblings to reunite with her parents. She is the fourth of five children. Her biggest artistic influences are Lucille Clifton, Nikki Giovanni and Jill Scott. She writes about love, life and family relationships.

She has lived in Halifax, N.S., Toronto, ON, Champs Fleur and St. Augustine, Trinidad, Detroit, MI and now Baltimore, MD.

Amour has two spoken word CDs, "Love's Journey" and "ilovemesomewords" —both have been reviewed by *Baltimore City Paper* and "ilovemesomewords" by *Baltimore Magazine*. Her award-winning poem, "Hermoso Negro" is published in Paterson Literary Review and she also has work in *Poet's Ink*. Amour has performed at festivals, retreats, bars and arts and cultural events in the U.S. and Canada. *Free to Be Me* is her first book of poetry.

"Love's Journey" and "ilovemesomewords" CDs are available at **www.cdbaby.com**

www.ingramcontent.com/pod-product-compliance
Lightning Source LLC
Chambersburg PA
CBHW072034060426
42449CB00010BA/2251